AF593896

Why Fings Went West

SOME MORE TITLES IN THE

Time Remembered

SERIES

Murder Must Appetize

H. R. F. KEATING

The Blackmailing of the Chancellor

KENNETH BOURNE

Pride, Prejudice & Proops

MARJORIE PROOPS

Keep Mum!

GEORGE BEGLEY

FRANK NORMAN

Why Fings Went West

A TIME REMEMBERED

London
LEMON TREE PRESS
1975

First Published in 1975 by
The Lemon Tree Press Ltd
Bassett Chambers, 27 Bedfordbury,
London WC2

ISBN 0 904291 03 0

Set in 11 on 12 Garamond and
printed in Great Britain by
Hollen Street Press Ltd
Slough, Berkshire

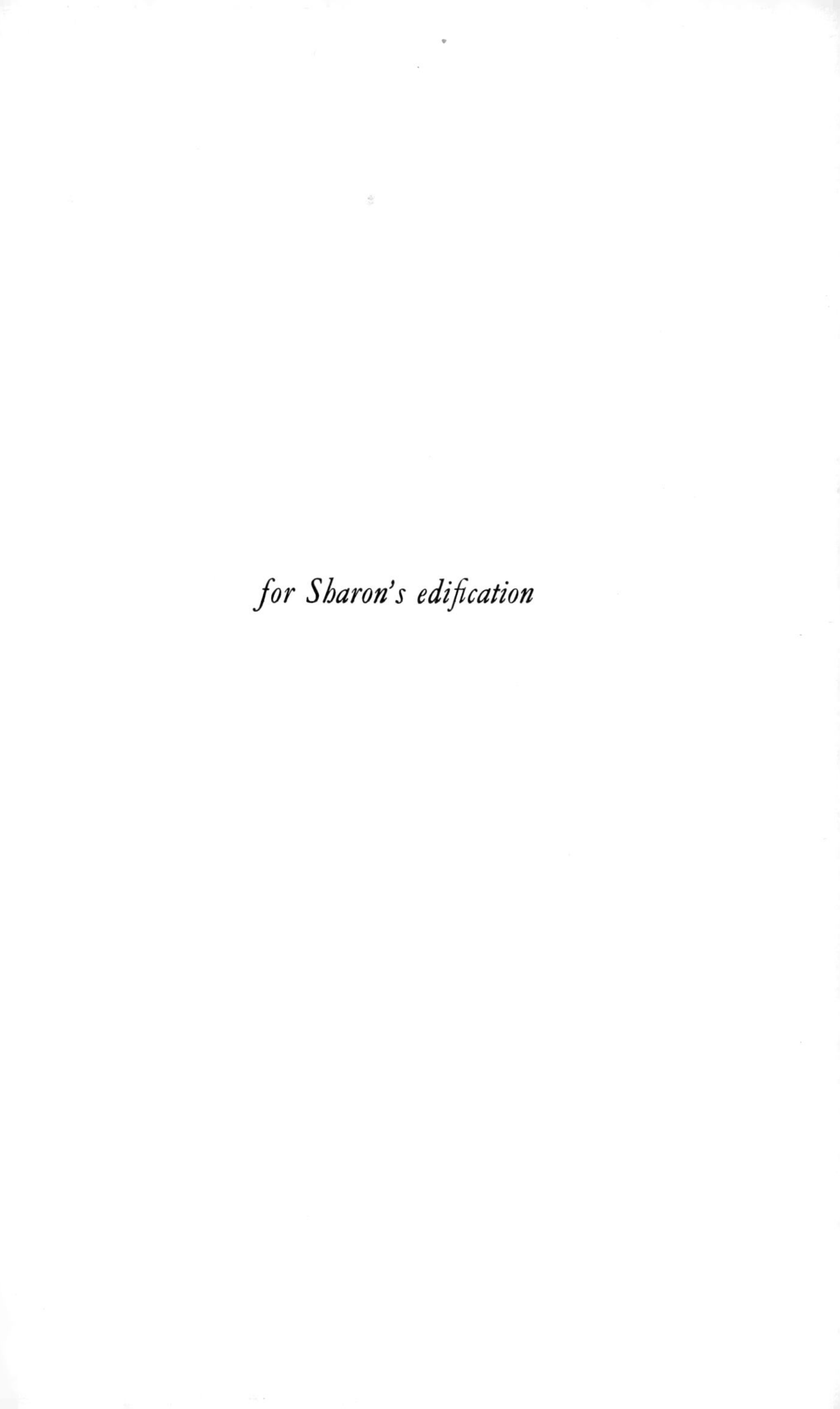

for Sharon's edification

Illustrations for this book have been selected from the following sources:

from left to right page 7 Donald Cooper: 8 Popperfoto: 10 Thomson Newspapers: 11 Associated Press/Houston Rogers: 12 AP: 14 AP: 15 AP: 19 Camera Press/Zoe Dominic: 20 Angus McBean/Jeff Vickers: 23 by courtesy of Punch: 25 Daily Express/Mark Gerson: 27 George Verjas/Herb Vickers: 28 by courtesy of Punch: 21 John Engstead: 33 The Guardian: 37 The London Express/by courtesy of Punch: 39 Wyndham's Theatre: 44 Camera Press: 47 Jeff Vickers: 53 AP: 54 & 55 AP: 60 Evening Standard: 63 Zoe Dominic: 71 Camera Press: 72 AP: 73 Vogue: 74 Black Star: 75 Popperfoto: 79 AP: 85 AP: 86 Ida Kar: 87 Pete Arthy/AP: 91 Mary Quant/Camera Press: 92 Zoe Dominic: 94 AP: 96 & 97 Thomson Newspapers: 98 Donald Cooper: 99 Donald Cooper: 100 Donald Cooper

Picture Research by Frank Norman, assisted by Olive Synge and Marsh Dunbar.

Welcome
to the
Show

Revolution in the air

Nineteen Fifty-six was the year of the Hungarian uprising and the Suez crisis. It was also the year when Khrushchev denounced the policies of Stalin. Revolution was in the air—C.N.D. and hundreds of sympathisers marched from Aldermaston to Trafalgar Square in protest against nuclear arms. Sydney Silverman's controversial bill for the abolition of the death penalty was passed in the Commons, but defeated in the Lords. Rock and Roll dominated the dance floors and rival gangs of Teddy boys and girls glowered at one another on opposite street corners. Young writers, many of whom had not even managed to scrape into grammar school, were laying their souls bare in N.W.3 eyries, North country hovels, Dublin pubs and elsewhere. They survived as best they could: dish washing for Joe Lyons, cement mixing for McAlpine or living off ideological girls for the sake of their art. Several soon-to-be-famous playwrights were serving out their apprenticeship with humble repertory companies.

But although the time bomb was already ticking and had been since 1953 when Joan Littlewood found a home for Theatre Workshop at the Theatre Royal, Stratford East, the outlook for aspiring young dramatists with revolutionary ideas continued to look grim. Seasoned web-spinners like Graham Greene, Terence Rattigan, Noel Coward and Agatha Christie were still

apest, October 1956

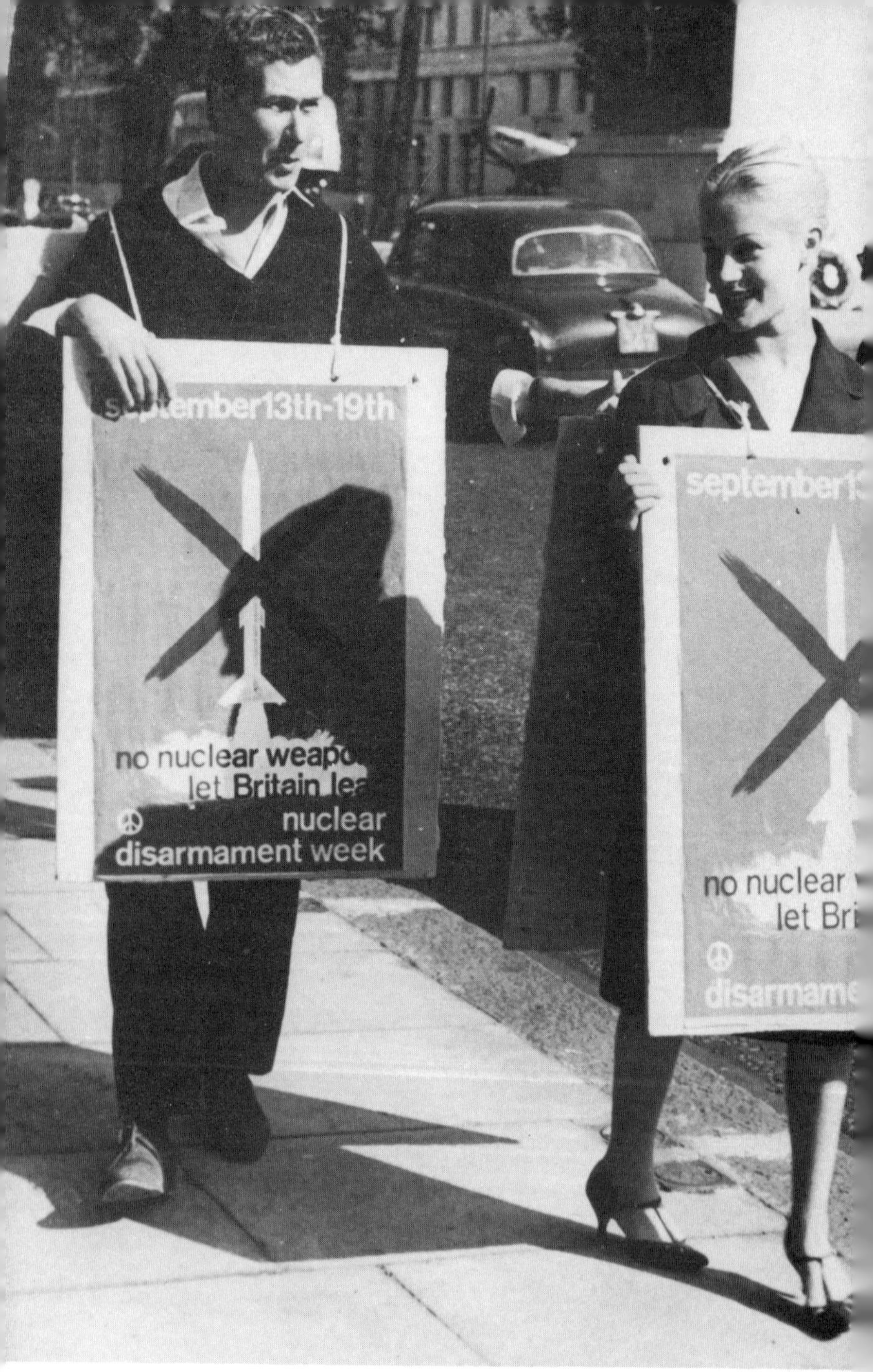

september13th-19th
no nuclear weapo
let Britain lea
nuclear
disarmament week
no nuclear
let Bri

Revolution in motion: *left* Osborne and Ure; *above* Vanessa Redgrave; *below* a scene from *Look Back in Anger*

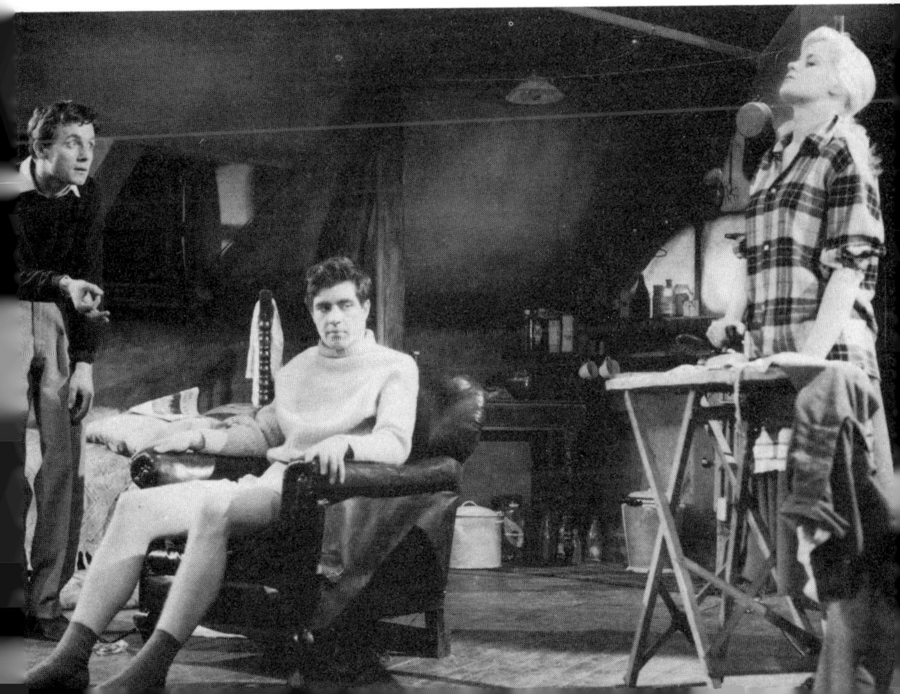

Doing the creep, *circa* 1956

churning out well-tailored drawing room comedies and middle class dramas with no aim other than to bring their plot to some kind of logical or illogical conclusion. Then on 8 May, 1956, the curtain rose on the first performance of John Osborne's *Look Back in Anger* at the Royal Court and the bomb exploded—the 'theatre revolution' was in motion. It was now the turn of the 'angry young men' to take to the stage with their 'kitchen sink' dramas. Raw talent took precedence over expertise and the well-spoken dialogue that had beguiled the middle-class diversion-seekers for so long gave way to the dialects of the proletariate. Drama school graduates with refined stage presence, and roses around their vowels, were overnight auditioning for roles they were ill-equipped to play and of which their mothers would not approve. When it survived the Lord Chamberlain's blue pencil: 'I fancy yuh double strong, darlin', so 'ow abaht a bit of the uvva?' became the language of the day and: 'Darling, I love you most awfully,' suddenly seemed as outmoded as the penny farthing.

Even the most reactionary of first-nighters would now be hard pushed to deny that the world premiere of *Look Back in Anger* was a decisive event in the history of English speaking theatre. But at the time there were many dissenters. In the national dailies the following morning there was not a single drama critic with the courage to go out on a limb or the perception to realise what he had witnessed. It was left to Kenneth Tynan, then theatre critic of *The Observer* and at the top of his form and influence, to make amends on Sunday with the following: 'I agree that *Look Back in Anger* is likely to remain a minority taste. What matters however, is the size of the minority. I estimate it at 6,733,000, which is the number of people in this country between twenty and thirty. . . . It is the best young play of its decade.'

Change in the air: Eden out . . . Mac in

On 24 May 1956, only a fortnight after John Osborne's opening salvo at the Royal Court, came the first London production of *The Quare Fellow* by Brendan Behan at the Theatre Royal, Stratford E.15 and with it came a K.O. punch for those meaningless West End entertainments that one critic called 'England through the eyes of the deb's mum.'

As unalike as chalk and cheese, the sudden emergence of Osborne and Behan, in that memorable summer, made a similar impact to that of Noel Coward

with *The Vortex* in 1924. The flood gates were open and over the next five or six years, at the rate of three or four a year, other young playwrights stepped out of the wings. To the Royal Court came Arnold Wesker with *The Kitchen*, *Chips With Everything* and the plays later known as *The Wesker Trilogy*, John Arden with *The Waters of Babylon*, *Live Like Pigs*, *Serjeant Musgrave's Dance* and others, Ann Jellicoe with *The Sport of My Mad Mother* and many more too numerous to list. To the Theatre Royal, Stratford E.15 came Shelagh Delaney with *A Taste of Honey*, Stephen Lewis with *Sparrer's Can't Sing*, Henry Chapman with *You Won't Always Be On Top* and me with a scruffy 48 page first draft of *Fings Ain't Wot They Used T'Be*. Making their mark elsewhere were, among others, Harold Pinter, John Mortimer and Peter Shaffer.

Salute General Joan!

The new theatre

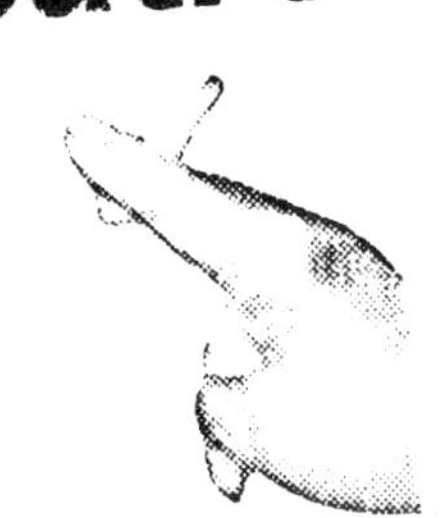

queen accuses

Littlewood's 'sparrows' are flying high

Joan Littlewood—the iron-willed genius

NEW TASTE OF WOT FINGS OUGHT T'BE DOWN ON LITTLEWOOD CORNER

Two-pronged assault

The two generals of the 'theatre revolution' were George Devine at the helm of the English Stage Company in Sloane Square and Joan Littlewood who presided over the Theatre Workshop at Stratford East. As unlike each other in their methods as the playwrights they attracted, there was one fundamental aim that they had in common—to stage the plays of new wave writers who would othewrise be deprived of a hearing.

Devine believed that a playwright's message should not be permitted to fall victim to a director's whim. The Royal Court was a 'writer's theatre' and, for good or ill, the text was allowed to roar over the foot-lights as forcefully as it did on the page. The alterations that were made to a playwright's work during rehearsal were not made lightly and never without proper consultation (a clause to this effect was even drafted into the Royal Court's standard play contract). It was left to the audience to decode the author's message. If they failed to do so and the play flopped, the playwright could at least console himself with the knowledge that the failure was largely his own.

No such luxuries were permitted at Theatre Workshop, however. The moment of a play's acceptance was very often the moment of departure from it. The journey from page to stage was fraught with hazards

Joan Littlewood, gleeful improviser. George Devine (and Olivier) sticking to the text

The Complaisant Lover, directed by Sir John Gielgud . . .
and suddenly—*Fings Ain't What They Used T'Be*

for the unwary playwright. Powerless to do anything about it, short of call the whole thing off, a forlorn author would sit hunched in the stalls and gaze up at a stage littered with discarded pages as Littlewood tore his play to bits with her bare hands, cut out the heart, gave it the kiss of life and tossed it to the assembled company of improvisers. With the raw material of adlibs she would then proceed to remodel the flesh in her own image.

But the legendary effectiveness of this 'method' of stagecraft was not without pitfalls. A well constructed play that, on the page, may have smacked of success could easily turn out to be a disaster on the boards. While a few pages of scrawled outline could be built into a 'smash hit' beyond the original innovator's wildest dreams.

The difficulties for a serious writer in a set-up like this are all too obvious. Most importantly there was the near impossibility of identification between what was originally on the page and what was being passed off on the stage as the author's work. This of course gave rise to a situation in which a playwright with a natural aptitude for drama would never discover how good he really was, while a writer with no knowledge of the theatre, but enough gumption to slap down an idea, would find himself saddled with a reputation out of all proportion to his actual talent.

WE DEFY YOU to resist his story—see P8

layabouts

Punch

Cultural Cell

FOLLOWING the success of *The Hostage*, whose author has done time, and *Fings ain't Wot They Used T'be*, whose author has done the same, managements are on the look-out for shows that will transfer into the West End direct from the concert halls of Pentonville, Brixton and the Scrubs.

UNDERWORLD COMES TO STRATFORD

Wenching

"TEN YEARS," said 38-year-old Norman, "is a long time inside or out. It's certainly the longest I've ever done any job, and now I want to be recognised not for what I was but for what I am—a pro writer."

The author as a young jailbird

Though it is already a matter of record, it is necessary to explain my own situation at this time. I was in Camp Hill prison on the Isle of Wight serving a three year sentence for bouncing cheques. There was no television in the 'nick' in those days and news from the outside world could only be gleaned from censored newspapers and primitive outlawed crystal-sets. I was vaguely aware that Colin Wilson, whom I'd seen around Soho during the post war years, had taken the literary world by storm with *The Outsider*. But I'd heard nothing of the theatre revolution that had taken place in Sloane Square and would probably have been moved neither one way nor the other if I had. In the spring of 1957, having served two thirds of my sentence, I was released from Camp Hill and a couple of months later, barely literate and with only my pettifogging criminal career to write about, I began work on my first book.

Like so many of my generation, who could muster the singleness of purpose to knock out a rough and ready manuscript, I had nothing to lose and everything to gain. There was, of course, nothing new in a young criminal opting out of the underworld and taking up the pen. Mark Benney and Jim Phelan had gone before and though I was unaware of it Brendan Behan was writing *Borstal Boy* at the same time that I was writing

Norman: 'nothing to lose and everything to gain'

Osborne: 'there are no more causes'

my own account of prison life, *Bang to Rights*. By accident or design, I never did discover which, both books were published on the same day in the autumn of the following year (1958). Over the next few years our paths were destined to cross many times and unedifying, if inevitable, comparisons were made of our work. With the solid success of his prison play *The Quare Fellow* already under his belt, Brendan was famous and I was still unknown. For easy identification and pigeonhole purposes, I was sometimes referred to in the press as the Cockney Brendan Behan and later the Cockney Jean Genet. I do not recall ever seeing the compliment reversed.

Jimmy Porter, the anti-hero of *Look Back In Anger*, had given the discontented post-war generation a slogan: 'There aren't any big, brave causes left'; it swept the country like a whirlwind. And malcontents of all kinds—artists, writers, photographers, musicians, actors, architects and even fashion designers—stormed the barricades of middle-class values and complacency. An image flashes into my mind as I write, of a bristly moustached retired army officer who one day marched into the foyer of the Royal Court armed with a riding crop and mouthing oaths. His deb daughter had run off with a working-class playwright and the old war-horse had resolved to 'Thrash the scoundrel to within an inch of his life!'

The 'movement' was eagerly embraced by the media and unpublished young writers had comparatively little difficulty in finding mentors.

The way of it in my own case was this.

Soon after my release from prison in April 1957 I got a job as a van driver for a wildly expensive Mayfair super-market and delivered groceries to the residences of the wealthy. On two occasions I was slipped a tip by ladies who, a year or two later, were to invite me around to their cocktail parties. After a

Soho: Kops, Bart and Norman get together

short period of sleeping around on the sofas of long suffering friends, I moved into a cheerless rabbit-hutch of a bed-sitter in Camden Town. But it was a fixed abode and, coupled with a weekly wage packet, I had provided myself with the modicum of security needed to give writing a whirl. Unable to spell or form sentences grammatically, and with no Gaelic blood in my veins to give me fire, I gingerly began to tap the keys of a recently acquired 1904 Olympia portable. In prison I had taken up the brush and become a Sunday painter. Now, with no other thought in my head than to slap the words down, almost as though I was speaking them, I became a Sunday writer.

Bernard Kops, a Soho friend from the starving late '40s, was the first person in the literary world to give me encouragement. His first play *The Hamlet of Stepney Green*, which he must have written during time off from dish-washing at The Mandrake club, was about to open at the Oxford Playhouse. On the first night, with several other Soho faces, I sat in the stalls and was as impressed at knowing someone who had actually had their play put on as I was by the piece itself. In the bar during the interval someone introduced me to W. H. Auden—I hadn't a clue who he was.

Bernard, a girl and I had once spent Christmas Day together in a freezing room at some nameless address. There was nothing to eat but a single egg, which we boiled and ate with three spoons. Making use of old ties, I prevailed upon Bernard to read the few pages I had written so far. And the next thing I knew he had tucked them into an envelope and addressed it to C. H. Rolph, the stalwart supporter of penal reform and contributor to the *New Statesman*. An enthusiastic letter came winging back by return of post in which Mr Rolph urged Bernard to encourage me to finish the book. A few months later it was done!

Bang to Rights. By FRANK NORMAN. & Warburg. 15s.

So far as I know, this is the first book life in an English prison to give voice

Prison from the Inside

"BANG TO RIGHTS"* is an account of two years Corrective Training served by Frank Norman in the prisons of Wandsworth, Chelmsford and Camp

Could change

Raymond Chandler writes of this five-time loser: "Because of his experiences and what he has had to endure because of what he has done, he is a potentially dangerous man, or so I think. But his talents as a writer ought to change all that, if he is properly recognised.

Bang to Rights

FRANK NORMAN
Foreword by Raymond Chandler

FRANK NORMAN
Stand on Me

'A natural comic writer. He has no self-pity, no desire to shock, exploit, heighten effects, teach or complain. Low life was his life ten years ago and he writes about it without sentimentality . . . This is farce in the high O. Henry manner.'—V. S. PRITCHETT *New Statesman*
16s.

Sent back

As a London blitz kid he was shunted from institution to institution ("I lived a very sheltered life"). He was twice adopted by foster-parents, twice sent back to the institution.

"I learned quicker than most," said Frank, hunching himself up in his white raincoat, "that life was the survival of the slickest.

This book is scrupulously unfair to the 'screws', the governors, the chaplains and others, but the sense of fairness is not given much nourishment among the predominantly young men in the criminal fringe, and Mr Norman has made me wonder how 'fair' I myself would be after a series of prison sentences that began with a 'suspected person' conviction. For

A Chandler as big as the Ritz

My luck continued to blossom. I was introduced to a publisher who rejected the book and a few weeks later another friend sent the MS to Stephen Spender who was at that time the editor of the highbrow monthly *Encounter*. He took 10,000 words of the MS and published them in the May 1958 edition of the magazine. *Encounter* in those days, many years before the revelation that it was backed by the C.I.A., was the most influential literary publication in the country and overnight I had arrived.

It was not the same kind of success as that enjoyed by Osborne, Pinter and Wilson. But to me it was the biggest step forward I had ever taken in my life. My name began to creep into the papers and I was introduced to celebrities at literary gatherings. A week after the extract of *Bang To Rights* had come out, Spender invited me to lunch at the Café Royal and said that Raymond Chandler (the creator of Philip Marlowe) had read my piece and had asked to meet me, so he would be joining us.

A slight commotion heralded Ray's arrival at the entrance of the grill-room. A few moments later he lurched into view and reeled across the room in our direction, leaving jogged elbows and soup-splattered shirt fronts in his wake. He was an elegantly dressed, elderly man of slightly less than average height with

'Taki' with Raymond Chandler

dishevelled grey hair, sympathetic eyes behind horn-rimmed spectacles, a crumpled polka dot bow tie and a merry smile. 'Howdy, scarface,' he quipped as we were introduced and beamed at me affectionately. I shook hands and returned his smile, then he slumped down in the chair next to me and ordered the waiter to bring him a plate of spaghetti. He was pretty drunk but I soon learned that this was his usual condition any time after ten or eleven in the morning. When the spaghetti arrived Ray promptly spilled the lot into his lap and I knew in a flash that we were going to be firm friends.

It wasn't until after lunch, as we parted company on the steps of the Ritz, that he mentioned how much he had enjoyed reading the *Bang To Rights* extract and asked me if I would let him read the rest of the manuscript. I agreed willingly and delivered it to him in his suite at the Ritz the following day. He was drunk as ever. I had not made a carbon, but I left it with him and went home fearing for its safety. I had given him the number of the coin box phone in the hall of the house where I lived and a couple of days later he rang up to say that he had read the manuscript and enjoyed it as much as the *Encounter* extract. He offered to write a foreword to the book when I found a publisher. I was delighted of course, but I had not at that time read any of his books and it was many years before I was able to grasp the true stature of the man I had impressed. And no less a time to realise that it was the relentless naiveté of my writing, coupled with an almost endearing lack of exposure to printed matter, that had impressed him.

Bang To Rights soon found a publisher and Ray contributed his promised foreword. It was the only time in his life that he assisted a budding writer in this particular way and there can be no denying that it helped considerably in drawing attention to the book.

'Barnardo' with Frank Norman

We met many times during the summer of 1958—there were meals at the Ritz, massive drinks and long conversations about life. One evening we went to see a play by Donald Ogden Stewart entitled *The Kidders*. I remember very little about the evening except that Ray fell asleep the moment the curtain rose. At the end of the first act there was a gun shot on stage and he awoke with a start and grunted: 'One gun shot doesn't make a play.' He was a lovely man. He died at his home in southern California the following year.

The notion of writing a play came to me almost by accident and was in no way connected with the revolution that John Osborne had set in motion. Indeed, if there was one thing that characterized the new wave playwrights of the fifties and sixties more than anything else, it was their individuality. Pinter, Arden, Wesker and the rest were Osborne's rivals not disciples.

A chance to brush up your slang . . .

New musical

THEATRE WORKSHOP, currently reviving **A Taste of Honey** at Stratford before it follows The Boy Friend into the Wyndhams Theatre, will be presenting what might be called a musical on February 17.

It will be **Fings Ain't Wot They Used T' Be**, the work of

Fings Ain't So Bad

A PLAY OF BRILLIANT, BAWDY IRREVERENCE

PLAY : Fings Ain't Wot They Used T'be
THEATRE : Garrick
By BERNARD LEVIN

Is this 'real life' —or is it plain dirt?

It is now the fashion among the "intellectuals," the arty-crafty and the unbelievably tiresome legion of The Dreadfully Young playwrights to sneer at who seek to reflect the good qualities of human beings.

Love with no tattered strings, kindness, hope, faith and common decency are no longer the thing.

Banished are the musicals such as came from the Lehars and the Novellos who gave us wonderful shows.

The beginning of Fings

Though I was not aware of it at the time, the seed of *Fings Ain't Wot They Used T'be*, was sown in an essay on London slang (with an emphasis on Cockney) that I published in *Encounter* in October 1958. It came to me at the time of writing the piece that a novel and effective way of handling the subject would be to present it in dialogue, in the form of several playlets accompanied by brief glossaries and explanations at the end of each. Stephen Spender was very pleased with the piece and thought that the dialogue was so 'splendid' that I ought to try my hand at writing a play. Not knowing enough about the theatre to realise the impossibility of embarking on such an enterprise, I wrote forty-eight pages of dialogue in one week and *Fings* was born. I originally saw it as a straight play and was vaguely aware that I should divide the action into three parts. This I did more by bulk than content and headed them Act 1, 2 and 3. I had no intention of submitting my efforts to a theatre management nor, indeed, did I have the slightest idea how such things were gone about. I put my pages away in a drawer, forgot about them, and commenced work on a second volume of memoirs, this time about my life and times in the Soho underworld.

A few months later the suggestion that I should write a play was made again. This time by Penelope

Shelagh Delaney, author of A Taste Of Honey, *has a small part in this play. With her here is James Booth as a Soho wide boy*

Gilliatt, who was then features editor of *Vogue*. (It was she who at about that time made the famous quip about the peace and quiet of an English Sunday morning being disturbed only by the sound of Harold Hobson, *The Sunday Times* drama critic, barking up the wrong tree. The reiteration of Spender's suggestion was sparked off by an article that Penelope had commissioned me to write for her magazine, and when I told her about *Fings* she enthusiastically asked to see it. It was she who shortly delivered it into the hands of Joan Littlewood.

It was some time before I had any word from Theatre Workshop and I don't honestly believe that I expected to hear from them at all. Then out of the blue Gerry Raffles, the company manager, wrote to say that both he and Joan were very keen on *Fings Ain't Wot They Used T'be* and that they would like to put it on sometime in the New Year—would I give him a ring and come down to Stratford to talk about it? I phoned immediately and the following week I made my first ever pilgrimage to the Theatre Royal E.15.

I knew of course that *A Taste of Honey* by Shelagh Delaney, the 20 year old girl from Salford, had started its life at Stratford and was now taking the West End by storm at Wyndham's. A year or so before she had been an usherette in her home town cinema, but now she was hailed on all sides as a genius. There had been reports in the press that she'd sold the film rights of her play for £20,000. And before her there had been Brendan Behan, the roaring Irish patriot, poet and playwright—who like me knew what it was to be locked in a cell, and also like me had written a book about it.

A week or two before I stepped over the threshold of the Theatre Royal, *The Hostage* had opened to rave reviews from the critics. Kenneth Tynan went out on a limb and declared that Brendan Behan stood a good

A Taste of Honey—'the best contemporary play now to be seen in London'—Graham Greene

chance of filling the place vacated by Sean O'Casey. It was certainly true that *The Quare Fellow* had already succeeded beyond the wildest expectation. No other recent Irish playwright had scored a success with

Royal Court realism: John Arden's *Serjeant Musgrave's Dance* and *Live Like Pigs*

West End audiences comparable with Brendan. Despite the global fame of W. B. Yeats, J. M. Synge and O'Casey, they had largely failed to engage the attention or support of the London entertainment-seekers. It would have been extremely rash to hope that *Fings* could achieve that same kind of success as *The Hostage* but there was always the possibility that it could be carried along in its wake. But I gave no thought to success or failure as I marched into the foyer of Littlewood's hotshop for the first time. I don't think my predecessors had either. It is only after a writer has tasted success that he begins to feel the need of it.

It was now the autumn of my first year as a published writer. *Bang to Rights* was in the bookshops. I'd been interviewed by Nancy Spain for the *Daily Express*, been chatted up on TV by Derek Hart, had paeans of praise showered on me by Gilbert Harding, knocked stomachs with a couple of upper-class girls and now here I stood on the threshold of the unknown.

THEATRE ROYAL
STRATFORD E.15
MARyland 5973

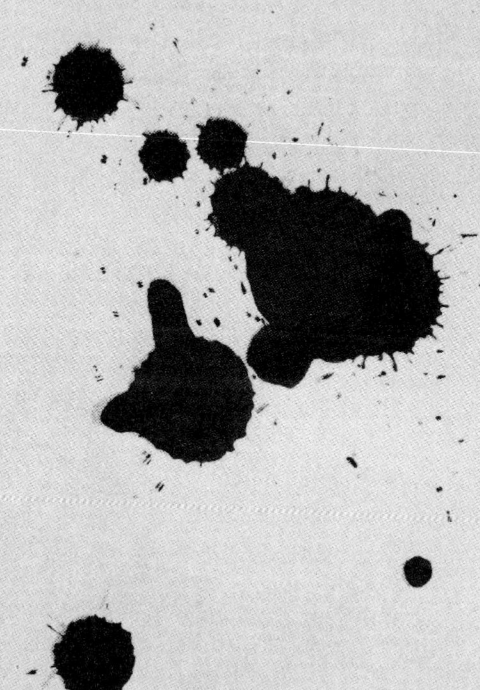

THEATRE WORKSHOP

presents

fings ain't wot they used t'be

by

FRANK NORMAN

with songs by LIONEL BART

dances by JEAN NEWLOVE

produced by **JOAN LITTLEWOOD**

setting by JOHN BURY

Theatre Workshop takes off

Back stage with Joan Littlewood

My impression of Joan Littlewood, when I met her for the first time backstage after the show, was of a solidly built sympathetic woman in a woolly hat, chain smoking Gauloises. She greeted me warmly, then we piled into Gerry Raffles' flashy American car and sped off to eat at a Chinese restaurant in Dockland. Over the meal Joan talked as though *Fings Ain't Wot They Used T'Be* was going to go into production the following morning, i.e.: 'What you've written is marvellous, but I don't think we ought to do it as a straight play, like all that old hat rubbish those West End managements put on. It should be a musical, or anyway have a few songs in it. I've met this wonderful nutcase called Lionel Bart, I've already talked to him about it and he's agreed to write some songs. What do you think, Frank?'

'It's a great idea.'

Rehearsals of the first production of *Fings* commenced in January of the following year. Lionel had already written a few songs or what he called 'top line and cord symbols' for the show. On the first morning the cast foregathered on stage and the peculiar process began. The famous extemporizing of the actors that had been infused into the text of *The Hostage* and *A Taste of Honey* was now permitted to run riot in *Fings*. With every day that passed my original conception of

Barbara Windsor and Toni Palmer—tarting up *Fing*

EVENING STANDARD

TUESDAY, MARCH 29, 1960

LONDONER'S DIARY

After the widespread criticism of the new £1 note, helpful Vicky here presents two new designs.

X CRISIS . . . BY JAK

9/3/1960
EVENING STANDARD

'Why do this to ME—Ain't I always treated you like my own flesh and blood'

NEWS CHRONICLE, WEDNESDAY, MARCH 9, 1960

Fings ain't wot they used t' be

the play seemed to drift further and further away, until eventually I was hardly able to identify with the antics on the stage at all. As the weeks went by more songs were added and once in a while I was called upon to write a few more pages of bad language. Then on Tuesday, 17 February 1959 the show opened and the rest is *inaccurate* history. In the books about the English theatre of this period that have come my way, there have been any number of discrepancies about exactly how many pages of *Fings Ain't Wot They Used T'be* there were for Joan Littlewood and her company to elaborate upon. They have ranged from less than a dozen to a 'scruffy' eighteen and one ungenerous columnist put it as low as five. As mentioned earlier, the true figure was forty-eight, and I wrote many more during rehearsals as well as a number of synopsis ideas for the songs. Like Brendan Behan and Shelagh Delaney, I had provided enough meat for a feast.

I did not deplore the means that have achieved this desirable end. The company has done some fine things in the past, but neither *A Taste of Honey* nor the current East End exhibit, **FINGS AIN'T WOT THEY USED T' BE**, is worthy of it. These are mildly interesting experiments with germs of ideas; nothing more.

YOU just can't get away from it. That's probably how **Frank Norman** is feeling about things these days.

BLOODSTAINS appear to spatter the front of the programme of Theatre Workshop's new production **Fings Ain't Wot They Used T'Be** at Stratford, East London. The setting is a shpieler, or gaming house, in Soho. Characters include an ex-Razor King of Mayfair, a man who sings of himself as "The Student Ponce," a couple of prostitutes.

Norman conquest of Soho

SURPRISING is the world of theatre. And no one more surprising in it than 20-year-old Shelagh Delaney, of Salford. Tonight, she goes on stage at the Stratford (East London) Theatre Royal . . . as an actress.

A remarkable thing, you may think, for a

BAWDY BUT BRILLIANT

Whether audiences like it or not, they are in "Fings ain' wot they used t'be" ...

'Monkeys flyin' rahnd the moon'

The bull-dozing of the well-mannered and decorative ideas of the old guard was well under way and by the dawn of the 'swinging '60s' a wide path had been cleared to the West End from the South West and from the East. The theatres of Charing Cross Road and Shaftesbury Avenue were soon awash with contemporary themes and earthy dialogue, the best of which must surely enter into what is permanent in English literature.

In the spring of 1960 there were no less than three Theatre Workshop productions running in the West End under the management of Donald Albery whose successful association with Gerry Raffles lasted well into the new decade with *Oh What A Lovely War* in the mid '60s. With the exception of the part he played in transferring Samuel Beckett's *Waiting For Godot* to the West End in the late fifties, Mr Albery will not admit to playing any significant role in the revolution that was taking place under his roofs. At Wyndham's there was the Littlewood (Irish jiggidy, jiggidy, jiggidy, jig-jig-jig) production of *The Hostage*. Jo, the heroine of *Taste of Honey*, now moved to the Criterion, continuing to sparkle with vitality as she told audiences that: 'I'm contemporary . . . aren't I? I really live at the same time as myself, don't I?' While at the Garrick a motley crew, in a straggley line across the

Miss Sam, a female rhesus, prepares for blast-off, 1960

From the
author's scrapbook
—snapshots of success

stage, were yelling a spirited reprise of '*Monkeys flyin' rahnd the moon/We'll be up there wiv 'em soon!/Fings ain't wot they used ter./Did the lot we used ter./Fings ain't wot they used t'be.*' Nor were they. Also with their names in lights during this period were Harold Pinter, J. P. Donleavy, John Mortimer, N. F. Simpson, Peter Shaffer, Arnold Wesker and the North country collaborators Keith Waternouse and Willis Hall. And with the 'new wave' drama, alongside the *eminences grises* of British theatre—Olivier, Gielgud, Guinness and Ashcroft—blossomed the exciting talents of Albert Finney, Peter O'Toole, James Booth, Tom Courtenay, Vanessa Redgrave and many more.

Stand on Me, by Frank Norman (Secker and Warburg, 16s.).

FRANK NORMAN is the author of "Bang to Rights," a best-selling autobiographical jail-bird's eye view of life in one of Her Majesty's prisons.

His musical, "Fings Ain't Wot They Used T'be," is currently competing on the London stage with the "World of Suzie Wong," "Irma la Douce," Brendan Behan's "Hostage" and a host of other plays in the contemporary bawding house school of drama.

Take a Butcher's . . .

Stand on Me. By FRANK NORMAN. *Secker & Warburg.* 16s.

FRANK NORMAN

Stand on Me

"Mr. Norman was about 17 when he drifted into being a lay-about at Number 86, a Soho kayf, lived with 'brasses' (tarts), stole, burgled, went to jail a few times, was cut up and emerged from all that, by some remarkable effort of will, to become a natural comic writer. He has no self-pity, no desire to shock, exploit, heighten effects, teach or complain. Low life was his life ten years ago and he writes about it without sentimentality . . . Mr. Norman is a born comic. . . . This is farce in the high O. Henry manner."

V. S. PRITCHETT, *New Statesman*

"Implacably authentic."

GEORGE MALCOLM THOMSON, *Evening Standard*

"This is better than any 'exposure' story."

Daily Telegraph

16s.

Stand on Me. By Frank Norman. Secker and Warburg. 16s.

Mr. Norman has made his contribution to penology with his *Bang to Rights*, a book that ought to be compulsory reading for anyone in a position to send a fellow man to corrective training. And now he makes his contribution to sub-cultural anthropology. He has, the blurb

The title of this book is Soho-ese for 'I'm telling you' or 'You can take my word for it,' and this is a further volume of autobiographi-
al gatherings from the author of Bang to
hts and Fings Aint Wot They Used T'Be.

the Charleston. Frank Norman recounted his prison experiences in "**Bank to Rights**" and now presents the seamier side of Soho life, again in the vernacular, in "**Stand On Me.**" . . . . . .

Chivalrous surrender ceremony

As if to give the Establishment's seal of approval to the renegade movement, the line-up at the *Evening Standard* 'Drama Award' formal dinner at the Savoy that year threw together as unlikely a contingent of bed-fellows as has ever been seen.

Charles Wintour then, as now, editor of the paper opened the proceedings with a speech in which he stressed:* 'The sheer range of shows being shown on the London stage at the moment is fantastic.' Then amid wild applause from a room packed with celebrities the presentations began.

Dorothy Tutin (best performance by an actress, in *Twelfth Night*) set the tone of the evening with a pretty acceptance speech: 'I want to thank you with all my heart for this lovely award,' she said, '. . . I feel very thrilled and encouraged.' Sir Alec Guinness and Rex Harrison (best performances by actors, in *Ross* and *Plantov* respectively) were 'happy' and 'thrilled' respectively and then it was the turn of the writers.

First to stride up to the podium to receive his weighty statuette was J. P. Donleavy, whom the judges had rated the most promising playwright of the year for his *Fairy Tales of New York*. 'I feel a little grey to look promising, though I'm glad to get a prize,' he

*Quotes from *Evening Standard* report, 24th January 1961

Evening Standard DRAMA AWARDS for 1960

BEST PERFORMANCES BY ACTORS

SIR ALEC GUINNESS

"Ross"

and

MR. REX HARRISON

"Platonov"

Presentation by SIR MICHAEL BALCON

BEST PERFORMANCE BY AN ACTRESS

MISS DOROTHY TUTIN

"Twelfth Night"

Presentation by DAME FLORA ROBSON

MOST PROMISING PLAYWRIGHT

MR. J. P. DONLEAVY

"Fairy Tales in New York"

Presentation by MR. WOLF MANKOWITZ

BEST PLAY OF THE YEAR

"THE CARETAKER"

Mr. Harold Pinter

Presentation by MR. PETER DAUBENY

BEST MUSICAL

"FINGS AIN'T WOT THEY USED T'BE"

Mr. Frank Norman

Presentation by MR. FRANKIE HOWERD

CHAIRMAN

Mr. Max Aitken,

Chairman of the Board of Directors, Beaverbrook Newspapers.

Mr. Charles Wintour, Editor of the Evening Standard, will propose the toast of The Theatre. **Sir Michael Redgrave** will respond.

(The Drama Award Statuettes were designed for the Evening Standard by Mr. Frank Dobson, R.A.)

said, and went back to his seat.

Few could have been surprised that Harold Pinter's *The Caretaker* had been unanimously voted best play of the year. In making the presentation, Peter Daubeny reminded us of Noel Coward's recent warning that '. . . accolades, prizes and critics are no good', but went on to describe *The Caretaker* as 'A rare plant' and Pinter as 'A master of carefully constructed rhetorical speeches revealing half-formed thoughts, impulses and motives in an indefinable atmosphere of menace, terror and sensuous disquiet.'

'I am very happy to receive this award,' said Pinter and fled.

Fings Ain't Wot They Used T'Be, carried off the award for the best musical. My name was called and I hurried to the microphone. 'It makes yuh very nervous, don't it?' I croaked. 'I ain't felt so nervous since I stood in the dock.'

Sir Michael Redgrave with his remarkable elocution, while replying to the toast of The Theatre, spoke at length about the 'new wave' theatre: 'We all agree that the new wave has hit the shore with resounding impact,' he said. 'The new wave is something we all want and welcome . . .'

THE OLD VICK'S DRAMA AWARDS

AFTER ONE YEAR THE CENSOR HAS SECOND THOUGHTS ABOUT 'FINGS'

FINGS AIN'T AS THEY MUST BE, SAYS CENSOR

Scarbrough cuts a show that made him laugh

"And the funny thing is," said actress **Miriam Karlin** yesterday, "the Lord Chamberlain has seen the play twice and thoroughly enjoyed it, to judge by his laughter.

BART'S RETORT

"Most of the material they want out has been used from the beginning. It isn't a question of a lot of things having crept into the script."

FRANK OF FINGS HAS AN ANSWER

'It's so stupid—I'm going back to bed'

'The reference to the Duchess of Argyll is to be omitted'

But despite critical acclaim and public support, the revolution still had many lingering and powerful enemies. The front runner and most feared, by playwrights and theatre managers alike, was Lord Scarborough, the Lord Chamberlain, and his assistant Lieut-Colonel Penn whose duties included those of censorship in the theatre. No play could be staged without first being submitted to the Lord Chamberlain's office at St James's Palace for his official seal of approval. Any deviation from the 'authorized manuscript' could result in prosecution and immediate closure. Answerable to no one for the, sometimes annihilating, decisions he made in slashing lines and occasionally entire scenes from a playwright's work, Lord Scarborough and his blue pencilling henchmen suppressed and damaged as many new plays as they could on behalf of society.

Few manuscripts emerged from the Lord Chamberlain's office entirely unscathed and several plays (John Osborne's *A Patriot For Me* among them) were refused a licence for performance. The only way that Osborne's play could circumvent this arbitrary decision was through the good will of the Royal Court who turned the Theatre Upstairs into a club in which paid-up members could *legally* see what they liked.

Osborne's *A Patriot for Me*

More broadsides at Aunt Edna: *The Sport of My Mad Mother*, Rita Tushingham in *The Knack*, Albert Finney in *The Lily White Boys*

Our own experience of the censor's ludicrous cuts in Theatre Workshop productions, while irritating, were not without humour. The script of *Fings* was delivered to St James's Palace prior to the West End production and returned in due course peppered with 'deleted expletives'—Jesus Christ, a number of sod-offs, piss-offs and bugger-offs to mention but a few. Also eliminated were lines like: 'I ain't got a pot t' piss in,' but strangest of all was his Lordship's objection to the word 'camp', which could perhaps best be described as a meaningless homosexual extravagance. If I can conjure up no better description of this word, how better placed was the Lord Chamberlain?

If criticism of the censor really only boils down to criticism of the office, rather than the officer, a letter that Colonel Penn wrote to the manager of the Garrick Theatre over a year after *Fings* had opened should have been enough to abolish the censor without delay. It read:

The Lord Chamberlain's Office,
St James's Palace, S.W.1.

7th February 1961

Dear Sir,

The Lord Chamberlain has received numerous complaints aginst the play 'Fings Ain't Wot They Used T'Be', in consequence of which he arranged for an inspection of the Garrick Theatre to be made on 1st February last.

It is reported to his Lordship that numerous unauthorized amendments to the allowed manuscript have been made, and I am to require you to revert to it at once, submitting for approval any alteration which you wish to make before continuing them in use.

In particular I am to draw your attention to the undernoted, none of which would have been allowed had they been submitted, and which I am to ask you to confirm by return of post have been removed from the play.

Act I

Indecent business of Rosie putting her hand up Red Hot's bottom.

The dialogue between Rosie and Bettie. 'You've got a cast iron stomach.' 'You've got to have in our business.'

The interior decorator is not to be played as a

Edward Bond's *Saved*. The Lord Chamberlain could no longer regret homosexual and his remark '. . . Excuse me dear, red plush, that's very camp, that is,' is to be omitted, as is the remark, 'I've strained meself.'

The builder's labourer is not to carry the plank of wood in the erotic place and at the erotic angle that he does, and the Lord Chamberlain wishes to be informed of the manner in which the plank is in future to be carried.

Act II

The reference to the Duchess of Argyll is to be omitted. Tosher, when examining Red Hot's bag, is not to put his hand on Rosie's bottom with finger aligned as he does at the moment.

The remark, 'Don't drink that stuff, it will rot your drawers,' is to be omitted.

Tosher is not to push Rosie backwards against the table when dancing in such a manner that her legs appear through his open legs in a manner indicative of copulation.

Yours faithfully,

The Licensee,
Garrick Theatre.

Glancing over this beautiful document today, with its salacious official language and parsimonious tone, it is hard to credit the rumpus it caused, and harder still to believe that it was composed in St James's Palace and not by some wag on the staff of *Private Eye*. I wonder now, as I did at the time, if Colonel Penn's main and gallant intention was the defence of the Duchess of Argyll. But at this late date I doubt if we shall ever know.

It's just as well things have changed

TUESDAY, February 17:,
First Night: "Fings Ain't Wot They Used t' Be," at Theatre Royal, Stratford. Jascha Horenstein conducts the Hallé Orchestra with Gina Bachauer at the Royal Festival Hall. Roy Budden conducts the Capriol Orchestra at the Wigmore Hall. Billiards. Wrestling.

In these days, it seems that the playwright's the thing . . .

The bad old days

UNTIL quite recently 26-year-old Frank Norman was getting first-hand knowledge of the more vicious side of the London Underworld.

But that's now a thing of the past and our Frank has rejoined the flock.

Don't worry

fter an early dinner. At the same time, the stars f the Thirties have lost their magic for the niddle-aged playgoers, they are too like themelves—leaden around the feet, silver around the emples, brassy around the eyes and brassière around the bust. The injections of monkey-gland which are intended to revive the old familiar plots only make them look more haggard—the farce about sex change, the romantic love story punctuated with dirty jokes, the melodrama updated with snippets of homosexuality and race prejudice, the family soap opera set among Chicago negroes. The West End managements still know nothing about art. But now they don't even know what they like.

From 'Beyond the Fringe', a friendly stab in the back

In 1961 the satirical revue *Beyond the Fringe*—which had started life as an undergraduate romp and had, the previous year, been seen at the Edinburgh Festival—came to London and was an overnight hit. With their devastating satire of political rhetoric and religious humbug, the linguistic comedy of Bennett, Cook, Miller and Moore soon became the smart set's favourite form of masochism. In their own intelligent and individual way these four good humoured young men from Oxbridge contributed as much to the revolutionary decade as any of the avant-garde playwrights. Indeed, such was their irreverence that the 'angry young men' came in for as much lampooning as the politicians—no one was immune, not even a scarfaced ex-jailbird who had so successfully excavated royalties from the slag-heap of his past.

Close on the heels of *Beyond the Fringe* came the B.B.C. TV Saturday night programme *That Was The Week That Was* and the breakthrough was complete. Using the same brand of satire as *Fringe*, *TW3* reached an audience of more than twelve million. Outraged politicians who had come in for some stick on Saturday night asked questions in Parliament. Dinner parties in S.W.1 and N.W.3 were broken into for an hour for the guests to gather around the box.

Lenny Bruce at The Establishment

Peter Cook camping it down; Frank Norman camping it u

Over halves of bitter in the local on Sunday morning the turtle-neck sweater and paisley cravat brigade gossiped delightedly, and not without a tinge of disbelief, about the scandalous antics that had taken place before their astonished eyes the night before.

The packed theatres of the West End had created a new and lively phenomenon in London society—the wealthy working class playwright, whose 'overnight successes'—as the *Daily Express* used to call them—were often made to appear even more spectacular in the gossip columns by the subtle deduction of a couple of years from their age and the addition of a couple of noughts to their estimated income.

From the rib of *Beyond the Fringe* also sprang *Private Eye* and The Establishment Club in Greek Street, Soho. Peter Cook from the cast of *Fringe* and a friend named Nick Luard were quick to realise the need of a place where like minded people from all walks of life could eat, drink, argue and take in a satirical cabaret. Premises were soon found and early in 1962 The Establishment threw open its doors to anyone who could afford the £10 membership. A princely sum in

are the
NTLEMEN?
FILM MAKERS
HAWKINS
IVESEY

Christine Keeler and Mandy Rice-Davies drive in style to the Old Bailey, 1963

those days, but there was no shortage of takers and within a few weeks it looked as though everyone in London had filled in a banker's order. The star attraction of the opening season was the American entertainer Lenny Bruce, who was imported for a month's performance.

The arrival of Lenny at The Establishment was (as one of his admirers put it) the cultural equivalent of the Suez crisis; the avant-garde flocked to see him like lemmings to the ocean

Considering the climate of the day, it was astonishing how many were shocked by his sick humour and the four-letter words with which he punctuated his routine. Milton Shulman and Kenneth Allsop (surprisingly) both gave him a roasting in their newspaper

Irving Allen, backer of *Fings*

columns and the management reckoned on at least a dozen walk-outs a house. Indeed, so *controversial* (the most over-used word of the decade) did Lenny's act become that it threatened friendships and marriages, and cut across the traditional lines of hip and square. His impact on the contemporary 'scene' was so great that Peter Cook tried to get him back for another season the following year, but after the public outrage that greeted his first visit the Home Office refused to allow him into the country on grounds that he was a danger to British morality.

But his supporters outnumbered his detractors and, to set the record straight, *The Observer* printed a list of some of the two factions.

Stayers-on

Alma Cogan
(been three times)
George Melly
(four times)
Ken Tynan
(three times)
Frank Norman
Christopher Logue
Hattie Jacques
Dannie Williams
(singer of 'Moon River')
Count Basie
Albert Finney
Tom Driberg
Lionel Bart

Walkers-out

Nancy Spain
John Osborne
Penelope Gilliatt
Professor Ayer and
Mrs Ayer (Dee Wells)
Siobhan McKenna
Billie Whitelaw
Lord Montagu

Some of the names of the 'walkers-out' are indeed surprising. But one can only agree with Aldous Huxley that 'people who are shocked are the very people who want to be shocked.'

WEST END SHOWS? THEY'RE FALSE RUBBISH, SAYS THE WOMAN WHO PRODUCED THREE HITS

THE British theatre has never had it so low. If it sinks any lower it will hit bed-rock with a crash from which it may never recover.

What was once family entertainment to which we could go as an scape from the stern reality of workaday life has given place to the osturings and crawlings of prostitutes and pimps who live by touting or their girl friends.

Romance, decency, wit and laughter have been pushed down the drain—and it is appalling what has come up.

Garbage

The family could go and did go, and they came away feeling refreshed and happier for an hour or two of escapism.

Demise of the Generals

With the death of George Devine in the mid '60s (many said from overwork) and Joan Littlewood's sudden departure from the Theatre Workshop a little earlier, the revolution had lost both of its generals. Why Joan decamped from Stratford is not really known. But it was generally felt that her left-wing principles would no longer permit her to churn out plays for West End managers to make huge profits out of. Whatever her reasons, disappear she did, as far away from the winking neon lights as boat, train and plane would carry her. Now and then a post card would arrive with an African or Indian stamp, but without her around to put our plays on, the Workshop dramatists were up the creek without a paddle. Admittedly, Shelagh Delaney had managed to secure a production of her new play *The Lion in Love* at the Royal Court in 1960, and there was a lot that was good in it. But it lacked the firm hand that Littlewood had placed on *A Taste of Honey* and it was not a popular success. As time has shown, a playwright of great promise was snuffed out—for she has written nothing for the theatre since.

With the resounding success of *The Hostage* on Broadway and the American publication of *Borstal Boy*, New York society had clutched the wild, disorderly, eloquent Brendan Behan to its bosom and he was already treading determinedly in the footsteps of Dylan Thomas. With so much bad company to fall into, songs to sing and bottles to empty, he found it

Littlewood goes out fighting

more and more difficult to concentrate on writing. Despite the rumours that he was applying himself to a new play entitled *Richard's Cork Leg*, anyone with half an eye could see that nothing short of a miracle would save him. When after his death the fragments of the manuscript were unearthed, the fiery Irish revolutionary who could once have boasted of possessing the same credentials as O'Casey and Synge had degenerated to:

ROSE: She's around behind.
MARIA: I know she has, but where is she?

and:

THE HERO: I have a great interest in French life, in French language and letters.
MARIA: (*Indignantly*) How dare you, how dare you mention such a thing.*

**Brendan Behan* by Ulick O'Connor

I too had a new play entitled *A Kayf Up West*, but no producer. However, I did have the consolation of *Fings Ain't Wot They Used T'be* still doing good business at the Garrick (it outran the rest of the Workshop productions by a year, then had a two-year tour of the provinces). In a less spectacular way than Brendan or Shelagh I too was beginning to feel the hangover of over-night success.

There were deeper problems that must have concerned all of the intelligent children of the revolution who had inadvertently come by more publicity and money than they had dreamed possible. Would they survive if their mentors lost interest in them? Does success inevitably corrupt or 'spoil' you and, if so, how quickly? And is the process so subtle that you do not notice it yourself?

As with alcohol, I suppose it depends on how strong your head is. Or, as Adlai Stevenson said of publicity: 'It's all right if you don't inhale.'

One of the most important contributing factors in the success of the 'new wave' drama was timing. *Look Back in Anger*, under the management of the newly formed English Stage Company, arrived at precisely the right moment and gave the flagging British theatre a much needed shot in the arm. It blazed the trail for all that came after. If *Anger* had not gone before, it is extremely doubtful if *Fings* with its pimps, tarts and bent coppers would ever have seen the light of day. But if three years after Osborne had set the ball rolling (1959) was exactly the right moment for *Fings Ain't Wot They Used T'Be*, five years later (1964) was too late for my second play *A Kayf Up West*. Tastes were changing; with films like *Lawrence of Arabia*, the £12 million *Cleopatra* with Elizabeth Taylor and Richard Burton, and the first of the James Bond movies, the cinema was regaining public support. And The Beatles had already made the Liverpool sound international.

In 1963, or thereabouts, Joan Littlewood returned from her travels and took up the reins at Stratford East once more. The company, more or less intact, were waiting, ready and eager to get to work, and from a radio programme compiled by Charles Chilton entitled *Oh What A Lovely War* an improvised work of genius was staged.

As much out of loyalty to me as any enthusiasm that she may have had for my new play, she eventually agreed to stage *A Kayf Up West*, in the spring of 1964. A first draft of the script had in fact been gathering dust in Littlewood's files since the early days of *Fings*. But despite a number of efforts that I had made to interest other managements in it, I'd sold only one option on it (now long lapsed) and had otherwise found no takers.

Kayf was a great rambling, panoramic, documentary of Soho's lower depths during the post war years. It had forty-six speaking parts, innumerable sets and one stage direction read: 'A troupe of West Indian immigrants dance on . . .' It is little wonder that I had failed to interest any West End managers in it. It wasn't even a musical!

The action of the play started on a main arterial road, moved to a café, a bombed house, the streets of Soho, Kew Gardens, Hyde Park, a Mayfair apartment, and to a prison. In listless mood with only thirteen actors doubling, trebling and even quadrupling to fill the forty-six roles we commenced rehearsals.

Forearmed by the experience of the Theatre Workshop production of *Fings*, my attitude towards Littlewood's methods of direction, particularly in regard to improvisation, had crystallised into a point of view which echoed that of Arnold Bennett: 'When I write a book I can devote as many hundreds, or indeed thousands, of words as I like to get into my reader's minds exactly how I want them to see my heroine. Should I be fool enough to write a play, all I can write is "Enter Millicent" and I am then in the hands of some damn tart who is sleeping with the manager.' But to my complete surprise, Joan Littlewood did not, on this occasion, encourage the cast to extemporize their parts to anywhere near the extent she had with *Fings*. By the end of the rehearsal period two thirds of the dialogue they spoke was mine.

A Kayf Up West opened on 10 March 1964 and was as big a flop as *Fings* had been a success. It was a sad evening and I was particularly sorry for a young actor named Edward Roscoe, who played my Candide-like hero Tommie White. It was a demanding role that called for Roscoe to be on stage throughout the entire performance. For a young actor just out of drama school and making his stage debut, the hostile notices must have been a shattering blow.

A programme note testified, not for the first time, that the Theatre Workshop's future was bleak: '. . . unless an adequate grant from the local borough councils or the Arts Council is forthcoming for the next financial year, *A Kayf Up West* will be the last Theatre Workshop production that the company have the financial resources to mount at the Theatre Royal.' The veiled plea was ignored by all the authorities and at the end of the run the company was disbanded. The revolutionary spark that had kindled some of the most spectacular successes of the decade had ignominiously fizzled out through lack of support. And the international fame of a tiny Victorian music hall theatre in the slums of East London would quickly fade while its bricks and mortar would, in a year or two, catch the greedy eye of the developers.

The man inside Brendan Behan

A number of people who were friends of Behan or who knew his work for the theatre yesterday gave THE OBSERVER their personal impressions of his more durable side, both as playwright and man.

THE DEATH of Brendan Behan on Friday may have left the popular impression that he was a man chiefly capable of drinking exploits and of getting into trouble with authority and the law.

Deckhand on collier

Mr Maurice Richardson, THE OBSERVER television critic, who knew Behan, said:

"I first met Brendan Behan in 1950 in Dublin, during Horse Show week. He was then 28, fresh-faced, very handsome, almost pretty. He was wearing nautical costume because he was supposed to be a deckhand on

Sense of freedom

Mr Frank Norman, the playwright, said: "I hate to see him emphasised so much as a mere boozer. He was, above all, a great humanitarian who would do anything for anybody. What helped as much as anything to kill him was his nine years in prison. If you aren't physically fit there you just go under."

Miss Joan Littlewood, of Theatre Workshop, said: "Brendan was caught between love for, and mockery of, obsolete myths. His personal suffering and loneliness gave the world some of the finest laughter medicine of the century. Already in his last notices the greatness of the man was undervalued.

"He was a fine scholar as well as a glorious clown, a man who translated Marlowe's verse into Irish and improvised his finest ballads for the street-sweepers and lonely vagrants of every city in the world. He squandered his life and his genius, but he took the world out on a spree with him. Theatre Workshop will put on 'The Quare Fellow' in his memory as soon as we can."

Mr Sean O'Casey, the playwright, said: "Brendan Behan was amiable and kind. He had no bitterness or venom or literary jealousy. Had he lived another 10 years he would have written more and perhaps better. It was horrible to think of a man of Behan's age dying, particularly when he had so much to offer."

Funeral at Glasnevin

On 20 March, ten days after the first night of *Kayf*, a stalwart Theatre Workshop actor named Howard Goorney, stepped up to the footlights and broke the news, to a thin house, that Brendan Behan had died in a Dublin Hospital during the performance.

Brendan and I had dogged each other's footsteps since the late '50s and it is strangely ironic that his death should have been announced from the stage of the Theatre Royal as the curtain fell on a play of mine. It was almost as though the lovable old Celtic necromancer was determined to have the last word.

A day or two later Joan Littlewood and I stood in the rain with the other mourners at Brendan's graveside in Glasnevin cemetery and watched his coffin, draped with the Tricolour, being lowered into the ground by the I.R.A. A boy bugler from the Fianna sounded the Last Post over the grave. The priest recited a decade of the Rosary in Irish. An old comrade at arms spoke the oration and quoted the old Republican song from *The Hostage:*

> "Wrap up me green jacket in a
> brown paper parcel.
> I will not need it now any more."

The Guard of Honour drew revolvers from holsters and fired a salute into the air—I was later told that the armoury had been taken to the cemetery in a baby's

Behan upstages the cast of *The Hostage*

BRENDAN BEHAN

Things fall apart: *A Kayf Up West* and Behan's funeral at Glasnevin pram. Afterwards everyone flocked back to the Dublin pubs and later came the fist fights.

In Gill's pub—where Brendan used to swear he had his first drink from his grandmother when he was six! —Joan and I were confronted by one of his brothers who said: 'Yous'll always find a welcome in Dublin—you're the only ones to come over to pay your last respects. Sure, there wasn't even a wreath from the West End theatre or anyone else in England who made their fortune from Brendan's writing.'

As the decade grew older, the hair of young men grew longer and girl's skirts grew shorter. The media's new pre-occupation was with the antics of 'pop groups' and the 'cult of youth'. Shoulder length hair became evidence enough to convict any youth of a drugs offence; the 'angry (not so) young men' of the theatre were pushed from the headlines.

WHAT SUCCESS MEANS—1

Nevertheless, they have, as the saying goes, struck it rich—principally, I think, because they have caught my colleagues at a uniquely propitious moment. Some of the barbs of the "angry young men" have drawn blood: perhaps the theatre does spend too much time on the problems of the well-heeled classes and is out of touch with the earthier elements of society.

This, I'm willing to bet, will soon have Princess Margaret sitting in the stalls!

A new film

His new play—which has not yet been produced is called "A Cayf Up West." He finished it in Spain last year. Down-to-earth London titles seem to head all Frank Norman's work. His film—starring Anthony Newley, Anne Aubrey and James Booth—is called "In The Nick," and will be released shortly.

—goodbye to the kayf...

The Royal kiss of success

However, in a submerged sort of way, accompanied by occasional twittering in the press, the theatre continued to go about its business. But as Establishment acceptance of 'kitchen sink' drama grew stronger and the playwrights more successful, that which had been outside Society was slowly sucked into it and in the process the movement was vanquished.

Princess Margaret and Mr Armstrong-Jones had been to see *Fings Ain't Wot They Used T'be*; the Queen went to *Beyond the Fringe* and is said to have laughed all the way through. Harold Pinter was given the C.B.E. and it is safe to assume that others were offered Royal honours but turned them down on ideological grounds. In any event there is hardly a playwright of the '50s and '60s of any note who does not have an Evening Standard Drama Award on his mantelpiece and probably a Tony, and an Encyclopedia Britannica Award as well.

Anger turned into civility, the teeth were drawn from the tiger, and the Osborne plays of the late '60s began to take on the characteristics of the middle-class Establishment of which he was now a fully paid-up member. Lounging in chintz covered armchairs, his suburban characters bellyache about the price of *rhubarb*, bang on, and on, and on in an unending monologue about the futility of their lives, the awful-

ness of the government and all the rest of it.

Osborne's verbiage culminated eventually in one character turning to the assembled company in *A Hotel in Amsterdam* and addressing them thus:

> '. . . Now I am boring. I am quite certainly the most boring man you have ever met in your lives. I see you are not going to contradict me, so I won't let you.'

What could the audience do but nod?

Paul Schofield in *A Hotel in Amsterdam*

Coward revivals prove the better part of valour

The West End managements whose contribution to the new wave drama had never really been more than providing a glamorous stage for plays that had already achieved critical approval elsewhere (usually the subsidised theatres) and from which huge profits could be derived, now closed their ranks and retreated to the safety of Shaw and Coward revivals.

Towards the end of the decade the Theatre Royal, Stratford, was 'dark' for long periods. The regime at the Royal Court had changed several times. Trend-making journalists who had jumped on the band-wagon earlier in the decade and had gleaned an immeasurable amount of kudos for themselves in lending their support to the revolution, hastily abandoned the sinking ship and began to tear down their idols—Osborne, Wesker, Delaney and the rest—with as much relish as they had built them up.

For the very qualities that the children of the revolution had once been praised they were now accused. Harold Hobson, never a staunch supporter of the 'new wave' even in its heyday, had wagged his finger as early as 1959: 'It is time that someone reminded our advanced dramatists that the principal function of the theatre is to give pleasure,' he had written in the *Sunday Times*. 'It is not the principal function of the theatre to strengthen peace, to improve morality, or

Coward revives: the Master attends his 70th birthday celebrations

to establish a social system. Churches, international associations and political parties already exist for these purposes.' But at least he was no turn-coat, unlike those who shared his opinions once their appetites for a new fad became jaded.

Young dramatists who, but a few years before, had not had two halfpennies to rub together, found themselves out in the cold again. The good years had brought temporary wealth and the bad brought income tax problems. Ideology had to be smothered and talent sold to the highest bidder in TV or Wardour Street.

Playwriting in a cold climate

A conversation over a glass of brandy with Dame Peggy Ashcroft, in November 1966, sparked off an idea in my mind of adapting *Bang to Rights* for the stage. Because of the size of the cast that would be needed for a prison play, I knew that it would stand no chance of a production in the commercial theatre. My only hope was to solicit the interest of one of the subsidized theatres. I dashed off a letter to Peter Hall at the Royal Shakespeare Company and in the fullness of time he commissioned the play.

Within three weeks I had completed the first draft which I entitled *Insideout* and sent it off to the RSC at the Aldwych Theatre. Though I did not realise it at the time, I had just embarked on the most frustrating *theatrical* experience of my career.

Whatever difficulties I may have had at the Theatre Workshop (in getting a reasonably accurate interpretation of my work), Joan Littlewood was never tardy in discussing a project to which she had committed herself. But the reverse, I soon discovered, was the case at the RSC. Indeed they were so busy telling me their troubles, when I was trying to tell them mine, that it was a full year before I could get anyone to hold still long enough to talk about *Insideout*, and it seemed like as long again before (without explanation) Peter Hall abandoned all hope of follow-

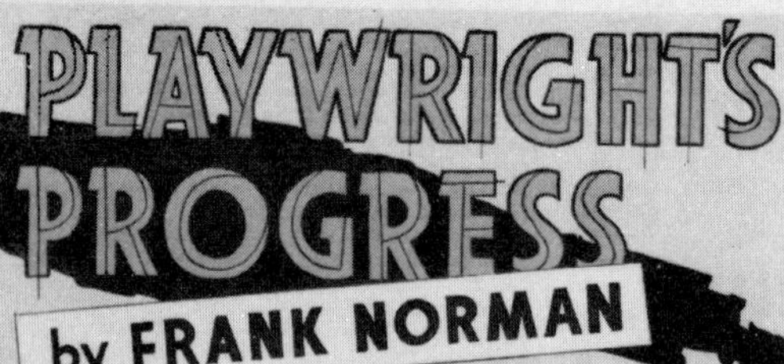

PLAYWRIGHT'S PROGRESS

by FRANK NORMAN

Drawn by Frank Bellamy

THREE YEARS AGO, FRANK NORMAN HAD DINNER WITH DAME PEGGY ASHCROFT.

WHY DON'T YOU TURN 'BANG TO RIGHTS' INTO A PLAY? I'LL TALK TO PETER HALL ABOUT IT IF YOU LIKE.

RIGHT! I'LL START WORK TOMORROW.

MEMORANDUM OF AGREEMENT made thi
3 day of March One Thousand Nine Hundred a
Sixty-seven

BETWEEN FRANK NORMAN care of Irene Josephy of 35 Craven Street London WC2 (hereinaft called 'the Author') of the one part

AND THE GOVERNORS of the Royal Shakespeare Theatre Stratford-upon-Avon Warwickshi (hereinafter called 'the Manager') of the other part

CONCERNING A PLAY at present entitled INSIDEOUT (hereinafter called 'the said Play') t be written by:-

FRANK NORMAN

NOW IT IS HEREBY AGREED AS FOLLOWS.-

1. THE AUTHOR hereby grants to the Manager the so exclusive licence to produce or cause to be produced t said Play in the English Language on the Professional throughout the United Kingdom Northern Ireland Republi Ireland Channel Islands Isle of Man British Colonies Possessions and Dominions (except Canada) and the Repu of South Africa (at non-segregated theatres ONLY) for period of FIVE YEARS so long as not less than Twenty-f Professional performances of the said Play are given i successive period of Twelve Months dating from the fir performance and so long as the Manager complies with a the other conditions herein.

2. a) THE MANAGER shall on the signing of this Agreement pay to the Author the sum of ONE HUNDRED AND FIFTY POUNDS which sum shall be on account of royaltie hereinafter mentioned and shall not be returnable in a event.

b) THE MANAGER shall on the delivery of the First Draft script of the said Play pay to the Author the sum of ONE HUNDRED AND FIFTY POUNDS which sum shal be on account of royalties hereinafter mentioned and shall not be returnable in any event.

c) THE MANAGER shall not later than EIGHT WEEKS from the date of receiving the Final Draft script noti the Author of its acceptability or otherwise.

d) IN THE EVENT of the Manager accepting the said Play for production at the Aldwych Theatre or elsewhere in the West End of London he shall pay to th Author the sum of ONE HUNDRED AND FIFTY POUNDS which s shall be on account of royalties hereinafter mentioned and shall not be returnable in any event.

e) IN THE EVENT of the Manager rejecting the said Play all rights shall revert to the Author.

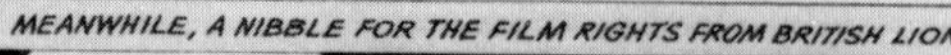

DISHEARTENED, FRANK SOUGHT RELAXATION AT THE CANNES FILM FESTIVAL IN THE SPRING OF 1969.

LINDSAY HERE AND TONY PAGE ARE TAKING OVER FROM BILL GASKILL AT THE ROYAL COURT IN THE AUTUMN.

WHY NOT HA A GO ?

How to get a new play produced – a three-year study in frustration

THE ROYAL SHAKESPEARE THEATRE

THE ALDWYCH THEATRE

Frank Norman, Esq.,
19 Netherhall Gardens,
Hampstead, N.W.3.

1st December, 1967

Dear Frank Norman,

Jeremy is now back and I have had a
Insideout with both him and Trevor.
the first draft that we saw c
play (which we all ...
to those marve...
Jeremy ...

– 2 –

I know how disappointing this will be to you and I'm truly sorry that we are not able to push our interest through to a more positive conclusion at this juncture. But neither do we wish to sit on the play, or block your chances of finding the help you need in some other quarter because of our own present inability to do what's necessary.

I do not honestly think you need worry about the contractual situation. I will ask Jeremy to drop you a note about it, but even if we still have a formal claim on it I would not wish to use this as a sanction to prevent you from now offering the play elsewhere.

If you do want to offer it elsewhere, but at a later date feel that you would like to talk to us again about it, please believe me when I say that we would be very happy if at that time we had the resources to work with you on it in the way that it should be worked on. Whatever you decide to do, I am glad that we were able to encourage you to write the play in the first place, and I hope that you yourself will not feel that it has been work in vain.

Very best wishes,

Yours sincerely,

Peter Hall

NGER

I ENJOYED IT A LOT, FRANK, BUT THE CAST IS TOO BIG FOR THE COURT.

Insideout by Frank Norman

ing up his interest in the play 'in the foreseeable future'.

I tried it on Ken Tynan, then Literary Manager of the National Theatre. He seemed to like it a lot and wrote saying: 'The dialogue is plain marvellous. What a terrible old reactionary you are! . . . But this is such a splendid change from prison plays in which everyone is either a lovable eccentric out of an Ealing comedy or the young Richard Attenborough weeping and misunderstood in a corner . . .' But there was no chance of a production of the play at the National. I had just about given up all hope when a chance meeting with Lindsay Anderson at the Cannes film festival led to a production of *Insideout* at the Royal Court in December 1969, under the direction of Ken Campbell —who, oddly enough, had been in the cast of *Fings* throughout its lengthy tour of the provinces.

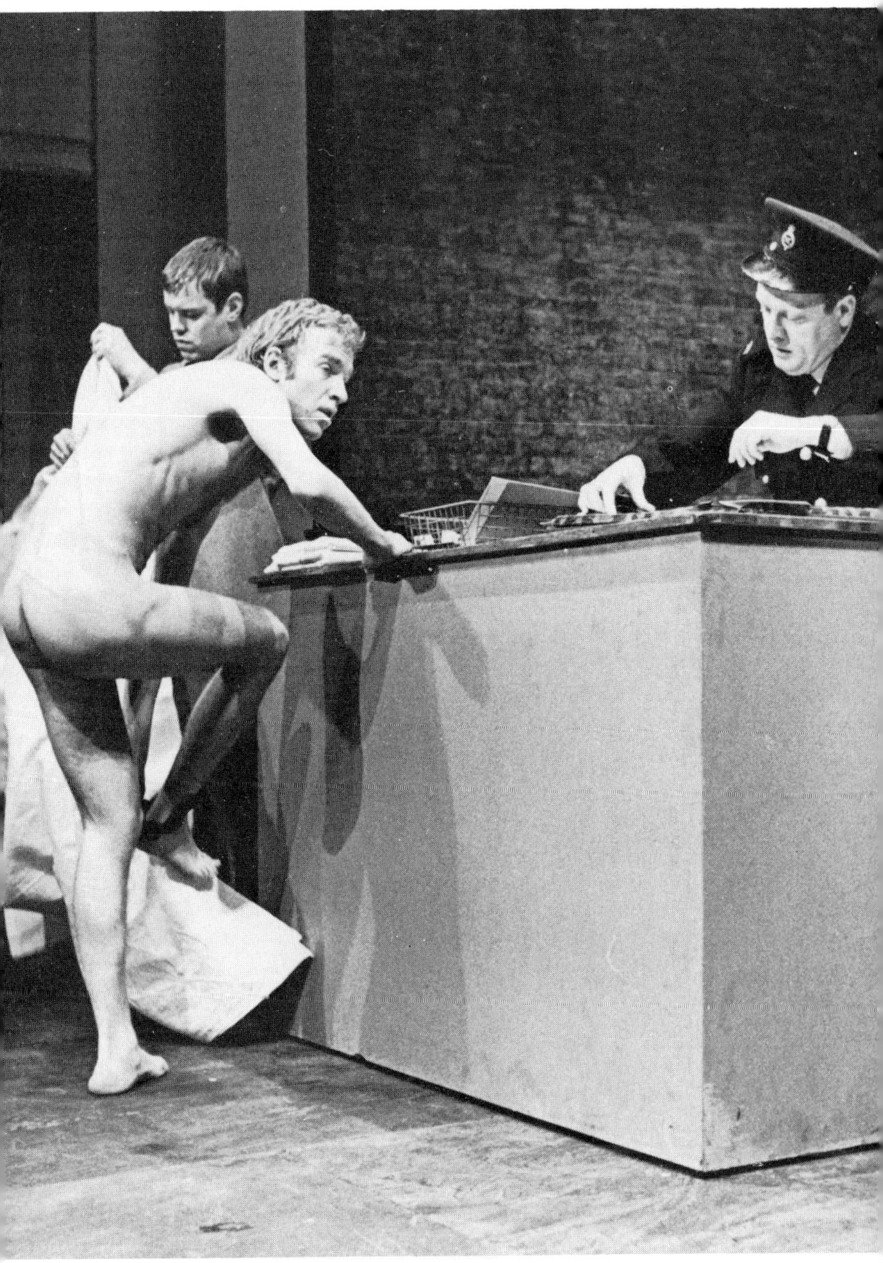

Full circle: the author, director and set designer of *Insideout* outside Wandsworth Prison

But if 'fings' had changed at Stratford they had changed no less in Sloane Square. The excitement and blind faith that what was going on on the stage was of world-shattering importance had been replaced by a gloomy atmosphere of resentment against drama critics and fear of failure. Some weeks before my play went into rehearsal the artistic managers of the English Stage Company had had a dispute with Hilary Spurling, the theatre critic of the *Spectator*, over what was called her 'Unilluminating attitude to our work'. Her name had been stricken from the free ticket list and to all intents and purposes she was banished from the theatre. The management's decision did not actually come to light until Mrs Spurling noticed that she had not been sent a complimentary ticket for David Storey's new play *The Contractor*, which immediately preceded *Insideout* at the Court. The incident caused a considerable flutter in the theatre world and a number of critics, led by Harold Hobson of the *Sunday Times*, announced that they would boycott the theatre while there was discrimination against an individual critic.

Carry on 'Mousetrap'!

In this unhappy atmosphere my play went into rehearsal and for four miserable, overstrained weeks I heard nothing but the bickering of discontented actors and cries of: 'Disaster! Disaster!' from the management. Nevertheless, my name went up in lights outside the theatre and despite the panic-stricken atmosphere that had haunted the production since the outset, I felt as much a part of the end of the decade as I had been of the beginning. In the event the critics who did turn up on the first night were, on the whole, favourable about *Insideout* and several of those who had boycotted the theatre came to see the play privately.

The decade was over, *The Mousetrap* was in its 18th year—see how it runs, and still no sign of the farmer's wife.

The Mousetrap—still going strong

About the Author

Frank Norman was born in 1930 in Bristol, and was brought up in the care of Dr. Barnardo's. On leaving the orphanage at the age of sixteen he was found a situation in a tomato nursery as a labourer, within months he ran away with a travelling fair and later drifted around London destitute and of no fixed abode. He began writing in 1957 and his first magazine article appeared in *Encounter* in May of the following year. He has published thirteen books, which include *Bang to Rights*, *Banana Boy*, *One of Our Own* and *Much Ado About Nuffink*. He is the author of the musical *Fings Ain't Wot They Used T'Be* and three other plays.

Also by Frank Norman

BANG TO RIGHTS
STAND ON ME
THE GUNTZ
SOHO NIGHT AND DAY
THE MONKEY PULLED HIS HAIR
BARNEY SNIP—ARTIST
BANANA BOY
NORMAN'S LONDON
LOCK 'EM UP AND COUNT 'EM
DODGEM-GREASER
THE LIVES OF FRANK NORMAN
ONE OF OUR OWN
MUCH ADO ABOUT NUFFINK
DOWN AND OUT IN HIGH SOCIETY

Plays

FINGS AIN'T WOT THEY USED T'BE
INSIDEOUT
A KAYF UP WEST
COSTA PACKET